MW01222630

Amsterdam Travel Guide

Thomas Leon

Amsterdam Travel Guide

Copyright © 2017 by Thomas Leon

Information contained within this book is for educational purposes only. Although the author and publisher have made every effort to ensure that the information in this book was correct at press time, the author and publisher do not assume and hereby disclaim any liability to any party for any loss, damage, or disruption caused by errors or omissions, whether such errors or omissions result from negligence, accident, or any other cause.

ISBN-13: 978-1974024261
ISBN-10: 1974024261

First Edition: July 2017
10 9 8 7 6 5 4 3 2 1

Thomas Leon

C O N T E N T S

3

Introduction

Welcome or "Welkom" in Dutch (don't worry that's about as much Dutch as you will need). My name is Thomas Leon. I've been traveling all over the globe for many years. I've taken bucket baths in India, eaten cobra's in Vietnam and gotten chased by a scary chicken in Nepal. While you won't experience any of that in Amsterdam (thankfully), this book will provide you with the ins and outs of the city so you're covered. I will show you:

- How to avoid trouble

- Where to shop on a budget

- Dutch delicacies to indulge in

- Weird things to do (to make your social media implode)

- All the amazing free festivals

And so much more...

Amsterdam is a glorious city, a cultural combination of art, food, music and loads of cool events. In fact, I'm not sure I've ever seen so many free festivals in any other country. Then there's the influx of concept shops, and places where you can eat and shop simultaneously (perfect for those who wish to save time). Art lovers will fall in love, post-teen backpackers will smoke some great herb and foodies won't know where to start— let alone finish.

When it comes to general knowledge about European countries, many of us fail when asked to think of at least 3 things about the Netherlands. Many can't think beyond those sexy wooden shoes called clogs. Is the Netherlands left in the dark due to the prominence of the larger bordering countries such as Belgium and Germany, or are coffee shops that sell pot brownies all it has to offer?

Here are a few interesting facts about the Netherlands to ignite your wanderlust:

- About 20% of the Netherlands is located below sea level.

- The Netherlands is the healthiest country in the world for diet, ranking above France and Switzerland. I wonder if it has anything to do with all those green plants growing everywhere...

- Gin was invented by the Dutch and introduced to the British.

- There are about 1000 windmills from 1890.

- The Netherlands has more bikes than people.

I know what you may be thinking, '*I don't need to visit Amsterdam—I've already seen clips of the city on YouTube.*'

Wrong! Amsterdam is a hotpot of curiosity and wonder. There are so many alleyways and canals to get lost in, each with the prospect of finding hidden gems, obscure trendy stores or craft beer bars. I had never thought there was more to the city than weed, the red-light district and windmills, until I visited and saw it for myself. I spent hours exploring vicariously, as if I was a 19th century spice trader.

What this book will cover?

With the help of this book, your trip to Amsterdam and the Netherlands is guaranteed to be awesome!

Before you ever set foot into Amsterdam, you will learn a few fascinating facts, how to stay out of trouble and a few things about Dutch culture to help you assimilate (if you wish to).

You will see what's on the menu in Amsterdam that will make you go ooh (pancakes), or eew (raw herring). You will find out the difference between a café and a coffee shop, and discover some unusual ways to experience fine dining, such as eating in the dark or enjoying home cooked meals in the home of a stranger!

Who says you need a map to get around when all the information you really need is in this book? Visit landmark locations for free, save money on transport, and immerse yourself in the local culture. If you have kids, the book even covers a few things for them to do, too!

Need somewhere to sleep? Ever thought about a houseboat? What about watching a movie inside a teepee? You can do all this and more in Amsterdam. Read on.

Amsterdam is home to all kinds of wondrous gifts, clothes, accessories and other items. If shopping is a necessary factor for enjoying your visit, you'll love this, as we showcase all the essential areas.

There is no shortage of events or entertainment opportunities in Amsterdam, whether you want to go to an underground party held in a basement, or visit a theater older than Canada. There is also an in-depth guide to all the free festivals that take place in the city, which you really don't want to miss.

If this is enough to get you intrigued and looking forward to a visit Amsterdam and the Netherlands, simply turn the page and let the journey begin!

Chapter 1: Interesting things about Amsterdam you probably didn't know

The capital of the Netherlands is not only a popular destination for caffeine-addicted stoners with a trust fund, but is a relaxed and refreshing hot spot for families as well (assuming they don't accidently walk into the red-light district).

Amsterdam is a compact city laced with inviting lanes, hidden gardens and avant-garde art. Most locations are next to a canal, (and a coffee shop by the way). You will find that exploring the city is relatively easy, since 90% of the Dutch population speaks English as a second language.

The city is colloquially known as Venice of the North, due to the remarkable architecture, the many idyllic canals that crisscross the city, and over 1,500 bridges from which you can take the ultimate selfie.

Other interesting things about the city:

• About 10,000 bikes are dredged out of the canals every year

• Amsterdam houses are built on wooden poles. Most of these were drilled in during the 17th century, which is why many Amsterdam houses tend to appear crooked.

• If you happen to stroll into the Red Light District, if you notice a room is lit with blue or purple it means the women might be more than just women.

• While Amsterdam has a traditional mayor, the city also has a night life mayor, a bike mayor and even a city poet.

• There are more women in Amsterdam than men. For every 100 men, there are about 145 women.

What's the difference between Holland and the Netherlands?

Holland is a region of the Netherland containing two provinces known as North-Holland and South-Holland. The most powerful and wealthiest region of the Netherlands, Holland is home to places like Amsterdam, Harrlem and Rotterdam.

The Dutch generally use the terms "Holland" and "the Netherlands" interchangeably, mostly when talking with foreign visitors. Some Dutch folk actually don't like it when "Holland" is used, as it refers to particular part of the country that may be different from their own region.

Dos and Don'ts

Do be alert for pickpockets.

Pickpockets in Amsterdam tend to hang around the train that runs from Schiphol International Airport to the city, which is usually occupied by tired tourists with too many bags. Make sure to remain alert, perhaps an expresso before boarding is in order! ATM's are also a prime spot for sneaky thieves, so due diligence is required, but you shouldn't worry as Amsterdam is generally considered a very safe city.

Don't worry so much about violent crime

This is less of a problem here than in other European cities. Typically, the worst thing to happen to tourists is falling victim to a pick pocket, or getting lost after eating too many space cakes.

Do ask any policemen that stop you for their

identification

Gangs may dress up as policemen and ask you a multitude of questions, while the other "cops" attempt to pick pocket you. Some might even go as far as to fake your arrest in order to search through your stuff when really they are stealing items while you aren't paying attention. In these situations, you should opt to ask for ID.

Don't pee on the streets

Peeing on the street is a popular pastime of drunken tourists, but in Amsterdam it's best to find a urinal. If caught by the police, you will have to pay a fine. This is easily avoided since there are urinals practically everywhere (canals don't count).

Do greet assistants on entering and leaving shops

The Dutch consider it rude not to greet assistants when entering a shop, so please don't aimlessly wander in and out without acknowledging their existence.

Don't drink alcohol on the streets

This is a big no-no and is also against the law. You will not only face a fine, but will also be made to empty your delicious beverage.

Do walk through "the 9 streets"

Located in the Jordan area, the 9 streets connect the Prinsengracht, Keizersgracht, and Herengracht. There are loads of great shops selling nearly anything imaginable.

Don't walk in the bike lanes

You don't want to get mowed down by a cyclist travelling 5 mph. These cyclists are pretty badass and they aren't going to stop for anyone, so if you hear "let op" beware, because this means "watch out" in Dutch.

Do rent a bike

Amsterdam is the kind of city where you can rent a bike and cycle around without fear of being hit by a vehicle. It is an inexpensive way to get around and see the city, plus think of the exercise. Take care and don't ride a bike at night without lights, the police won't tolerate it.

Don't let your parking meter expire

If you plan on driving in Amsterdam always pay the parking fees. Getting busted results in some hefty fines.

Do save 16 Euros and skip the Heineken Experience

You can literally buy 8 Heinekens at any bar for the

price of entry or alternatively, 4 craft beers AND a tour of a microbrewery instead. There are loads of microbreweries to choose from too, so keep an open mind.

Don't be a bad tourist

No yelling late at night or smoking pot on public sidewalks please, this will infuriate the locals.

Chapter 2: Things to eat

Dutch cheese

Dutch cuisine is fairly simple, based mostly on vegetables and small portions of meat. For breakfast and lunch, the Dutch enjoy bread with luscious toppings of cheese, while dinner is more focused on meat and potatoes with some seasonal vegetables added in to make things just a bit more exciting.

The common diet in the Netherlands is high in carbohydrates, fat and dairy products. If you don't take into consideration any particular refinements, the cuisine is often described as rustic in nature, though during holidays, there are some special foods. Dutch colonies, such as the Dutch East Indies, have influenced the diet significantly in major cities, giving a more international feel to the food. Let's have a look at some dishes you MUST try when in the Netherlands.

Bitterballen

Bitterballen is a common snack served in Dutch pubs, they are deep fried meatballs and are usually served with mustard for dipping. Perfect for when you have had way too many 8% Belgian beers.

Thick Dutch fries

These fries might be called patat or frites on menus and are usually served in a piping hot paper cone covered in tasty toppings. If you want something a little unusual, try out 'patatje oorlog' for a dollop of peanut satay sauce, mayo and onions, or a 'patat speciaal' for a mix of curry ketchup, mayonnaise and onions.

Stroopwafel

Imagine two thin waffles stuck together with a layer of sweet syrup, yummy! Stroopwafels are available in bakeries all over the city and taste amazing hot out of the iron.

Raw Herring

This specialty certainly seems daunting but it's worth a try when in Amsterdam. Ask for a 'broodje haring' to get the fish served in a small sandwich with pickles and fresh onions. The best time to try raw herring is usually between May and July when the herring is said to be at its sweetest.

Croquettes from a vending machine

Hole-in-the-wall cafés are an actual thing in Amsterdam, and a popular snack among the Dutch is croquettes. Visit any FEBO and there is an array of delectable snacks behind glass doors. These unique vending machines are probably a godsend to stoner tourists.

Kibbeling

Kibberling is also fish but fortunately not raw, the dish is a battered and deep fried cod, served with a mayo-herb sauce and lemon. Kibberling is found in street markets or food trucks.

Poffertjes

These are fluffy round balls of sugary goodness, made from batter and served in restaurants and pancake houses. You can also opt to buy them from street market vendors. These are even more buttery and sprinkled with powdered sugar.

Cheese

Cheese is so huge in the Netherlands that houses might as well be built from it. Amsterdam has many 'kaas' stores where you can taste a variety of different cheeses, so put on your party hat. Alternatively, pop by the cheese museum (that's right, they really love cheese that much) or visit the Reypenaer Tasting Room for a guide to their award-winning cheese.

Tompouce

Tompounce is a rectangular pastry with a cream filling and a layer of pink icing on top. It's said to be named after a dwarf whose name was Tom Pounce.

The icing is turned bright orange on king's day.

Dutch licorice

Apparently, the Netherlands has the highest consumption of licorice in the whole world. However, this version is more salty and known as 'drop'. So if you get offered some licorice, you might want to give it a try.

Snert

A thick pea soup with celery, onions, pork and leek. Even though it sounds odd, it tastes amazing. Usually consumed during the winter, it is traditionally served by street vendors to ice skaters on frozen canals.

Indonesian Rijstaffel

The Indonesian influence can be found everywhere around Amsterdam and it is highly recommended to try a culinary tour at an Indonesian restaurant. The combination of Dutch-Indish dishes will leave you astonished. Order a Rijstaffel (rice table) and prepare to be presented with a medley of small dishes that were created during the times of Dutch colonization.

Stamppot

This dish translates as 'mash pot' and is essentially mashed potatoes with vegetables. It may also include sauerkraut, carrot or onion, and is accompanied with a thick sausage to gorge on.

Ontbijtkoek

Probably one of the hardest things you will come across to pronounce while in the Netherlands, this ginger cake comes in loaves and is so thick that one slice should satisfy you immediately. The name translates as 'breakfast cake' though it is delicious any time of the day.

Oliebollen

These are deep fried dumplings dusted in powdered sugar. There are sometimes fruit pieces thrown in. Translated as 'oil balls,' these only come out during New Year's Eve.

You Must Eat At These Places

A brief guide to weed and coffee

It is no secret that coffee plays an integral part of Dutch culture, but what may be surprising for some is just how much is available, and the wide variety of flavors the coffee comes in. It is important to remember that there is a difference between a cafe and a coffee shop, one of which is where people use weed recreationally.

The majority of the coffee shops are located in the Old Center, and look like normal cafés. They are prevented from advertising, so you must check out their menu. If you do plan on buying some weed, handle with care as it is extremely potent. Coffee shops open around 10am and close at midnight. Let's check out some of the quintessential places to get coffee in Amsterdam.

Coffee shops to check out are listed below. To be clear, these are where to go to smoke weed.

Make bong buddies at Bij (boerejongens)

Located: Bonairestraat 78, 1058 XL Amsterdam, Canal Belt Area & West

Boerejongens translates as 'farmer boys' in Dutch and this chain has 3 coffee shops in the city. This popular coffee shop offers high quality products combined with a lot of expertise at very affordable prices.

Visit the award-winning Barney's Coffee shop

Located: Haarlemmerstraat 102, 1013 EW Amsterdam, Westerpark Area

Barney's is renowned among locals and tourists alike, winning the "High Times Cup" award several times. Not only is this reputable coffee shop good for green, they also serve an excellent breakfast, lunch and dinner. You might find yourself practically living there.

Find the best green at GreenHouse Coffee shop

Located: Oudezijds Voorburgwal 191, 1012 EW Amsterdam, Old Center

While Barney's coffee shop has won several High Times Cannabis Cups, GreenHouse supersedes this with a staggering 38 awards. A popular hang-out spot for travelers vacationing in Amsterdam, what's really fascinating is their wall of fame showcasing a collection of celebrities who have visited the site. The location is next to the red light district so maybe best to leave before dark before the bright lights scare or confuse you.

Watch boats pass by at Amnesia

Located: Herengracht 133, 1015 BG Amsterdam, Canal Belt Area

Though Amnesia is a quaint coffee shop, the interior is full of stunning lights and ambient music to relax to. The coffee shop has a unique menu focused on 100% organic produce and it's a fine location to idly sit and watch passing boats.

Hang out at Dampkring coffee shop where the Ocean 12 film crew spent time

Located: Handboogstraat 29, 1012 XM Amsterdam, Canal Belt Area

That's right. During filming in Amsterdam, the film crew of Oceans 12 was known to visit this coffee shop. This world famous coffee shop is spacious inside, and serves excellent drinks at a standard competitive price.

Learn about the huge reputation of the tiny Grey Area Coffee Shop

Located: Oude Leliestraat 2, 1015 AW Amsterdam, Canal Belt Area

Grey Area is a tiny spot but with a big reputation. A favorite location for Americans, the friendly and knowledgeable staff will make you feel right at home.

Over the years, Grey Area coffee shop has had several high-profile celebrities as customers such as Snoop Dogg, Deftones, Lou Reed and many more.

Discover the very first ever coffee shop in Amsterdam

Located: Leidseplein 15, 1017 PS Amsterdam, Canal Belt Area

Probably the most well-known coffee shop in Amsterdam thanks to the central location at Leidseplein. Though ironically, the building is a former Amsterdam police station. The Bulldog is actually a chain of Bulldogs spread around the city center. The Bulldog No. 90 (Oudezijds Voorburgwal 88) was the first coffee shop in Amsterdam and laid the benchmark for the existing coffee shops in Amsterdam. Visiting Amsterdam for a few days and looking for a hotel near Amsterdam coffee shops? The Bulldog Hotel Amsterdam is located along a canal, you find it at the Oudezijds Voorburgwal 220.

Intriguing restaurants to try out

Amsterdam is a pioneer when it comes to unique dining experiences. If you can smoke weed in coffee shops, you might wonder what can happen when you go out for food. Here's a selection of weird and wonderful restaurants to consider while in Amsterdam.

Eat on a secret Island

During the summer in Amsterdam, you can take a boat to a nearby deserted island with the prospects of a four-course meal inside a greenhouse especially made for the occasion. Vuurtoreneiland's Zommerrestaurant is only available during the summer, so be sure to check out the pop-up restaurant before it goes.

Fresh food from garden to plate at Restaurant de

Kas

The menu at this restaurant changes daily based on what's been freshly picked from their garden. The restaurant feels like a massive greenhouse, with the building dating back to the 1920s, used by the Amsterdam community as a sort of public greenhouse.

Home-cooked meals minus the clearing up

Living room restaurants are an upcoming trend in Amsterdam, providing opportunities to mingle with strangers, enjoy dishes made right from the chef's home, and get involved in local culture. One of the most popular to visit is Saskia's living room restaurant. It's recommended to book in advance, but it's it full you can find several others online.

Join a workshop that merges cooking and art

De Culinaire Werkplaats encourages participants to create dishes inspired by themes such as 'black,' 'honesty,' and 'water.' This restaurant is focused on ensuring that ingredients are organically produced, plus only fair-trade and high-quality ingredients are used. The owners are constantly looking to push the boundaries of modern cuisine, and even new ways of eating. At the end of the meal, you also get the flexibility to decide on what to pay.

REM Eiland: Pirate radio station turned restaurant

Who would turn down the opportunity for dining 22 meters above water inside a radio station—a pirate radio station, that is. The restaurant is named after the REM law that shut down the station back in 1964, and now REM Eiland is one of Amsterdam's more unusual places for foodies, tourists and locals.

Gorge on Gourmet cuisine while on a train

Panorama Rail Restaurant takes you through Amsterdam's hidden villages and idyllic landscapes while you help yourself to a four-course meal, it's a win-win. The 1960s styled carriages will make you feel like you stepped back in time, and the three-hour journey passes through some of the Netherlands most iconic and notable spots such as Rotterdam, Harrlem and Den Haag.

Dining in the dark

Ctaste is very different from most restaurants, in that you sit in total darkness. The concept behind the restaurant is that by eliminating one of your senses, your other senses will become heightened. The primary aim is that diner's will take even more pleasure in the meal.

Ever looked at a menu where dishes are based on temperature?

Restaurant C developed their menu in order of temperature zones, highlighting their uncanny cooking techniques. There is such a diverse range of dishes to choose from, such as 0-20°C gazpacho, 40-80°C slow-cooked pork and 100°C steamed lobster. The conflicting temperatures are thought to create a special level of flavor.

Drinking & Nightlife

If you like beer, you are in for a treat, as Amsterdam has many microbreweries for the craft beer connoisseur, as well as many local brands to try. Locals enjoy strong Belgian beers such as Duvel or Westmalle Triple and there's also Witbier (white beer) that's consumed during the summer, accompanied with a slice of lemon. Darker, sweeter beer known as Bokbier comes out later in the fall.

If you aren't a big fan of beer, fortunately there are options such as Jenever, aka Dutch gin. A common mixture of this drink and beer creates kopstoot (head butt) though few people can handle two or three of these.

Three bars in one

Even though the Tara bar is essentially a British pub, with seven rooms, three bars and two sidewalk terraces to choose from, this bar is optimized to fit in at least a few dozen elephants. Prices might sting you however, so it might be worth visiting for one or two beverages before moving on.

50+ Belgian beers under one roof

Café Belgique's dark interior is decorated in bottles and beer placards, and there's not much room to swing a cat, but this only amplifies its cozy and intimate atmosphere. The location of the bar is perfect, central in the city and at night, many locals squeeze in to swig one of the many Belgian beers on offer.

A microbrewery inside a windmill

While the location is a little trek out of the tourist territory, and it closes at 8pm, the experience itself compensates. This is also the only windmill in the city. This is one of the most loved microbreweries in Amsterdam, and it is easy to understand why. Hand-crafted beers on tap, a convivial atmosphere that makes you feel at home, and plenty of cheese and sausage platters to keep you busy.

Nightclubs for later

Amsterdam's thriving nightlife caters to every type of tourist you can think of. From raw warehouses to swanky nightspots or even an elusive basement, there's no limit on where to go. World famous DJs pump out everything from techno, dub step, hip-hop, deep house and trance. Amsterdam is the world's biggest promoter of dance music and the city overflows with locations to pump your fists until daylight. Here are a few clubs in Amsterdam guaranteed for an exceptional night.

Get some shelter

Shelter is one of the newest additions to Amsterdam's club scene, located in the north side of the city. The venue is in the basement of the former shell tower and what's interesting is that on club nights, the venue opens a hatch allowing visitors to clamber inside. The club also has a 24-hour permit, so prepare to dance well into the morning.

A club night focused on more than just the music

The Tolhuistuin holds a club night known as Progress bar, what makes this night stand out is that it's focused on social and political awareness. The event combines talks, screenings, performances and clubbing all into one night. Progress bar is found inside the canteen of the old Shell factory, here club-goers get to experience music, theater and exhibitions through the events experimental offerings.

Squat turned club nights

OT301 is a multi-story building that holds a gallery space, club, vegan restaurant, cinema and underground dance room. The building used to be home to squatters, but now it's been upgraded for featuring intrinsic club nights, concerts and collaborations.

Dance while you pee

Club NYX is considered a little freer than the rest

of the clubs in Amsterdam. It has a three-floor venue with the third floor being the toilet. Inside the toilet is a DJ booth, great for when you want to dance and pee at the same time. The club is decorated in thought-provoking neon lights and you can't escape them. There is a regular night known as Vogue where everyone dresses in wigs and big dresses, and comes to dance. This is certainly something you might want to experience at least once.

Chapter 3: Exploring the city

Amsterdam was founded as a little fishing village back in the 13th century has only progressed further through trade since then. Amsterdam managed to secure many products such as wheat, diamonds and guns through exclusive trading rights, allowing the city to become one of the richest in the world (in the 17th century anyway). While there was much business going on, the Dutch people were fighting a war against Spanish imperial rule, in a war lasting for 80 years. They won the war in 1648, becoming the only republic in Western Europe at that time. Though peace didn't last long, as France attempted to invade in 1975 and stayed for 20 years, altering the Dutch language and culture with a French influence. In 1813, the French finally left and the Dutch decided to establish a constitutional monarchy, and since the Oranges family was the most well-respected and noble, they became royals.

In 1940, Hitler came along and decided to occupy the country for 5 years, which had a devastating effect on the Jewish community (losing 10% of their population).

After the war, Amsterdam swiftly blossomed from a trade city to a service-based city. Drastic changes to the police force and many liberalization movements in the 60s made Amsterdam propel economically.

Free Things to do

What is the first thing you need to do in Amsterdam? You might say visiting a coffee shop, but there is actually something more vital to get... a city card.

You can actually order a city card online before your trip, and using this card allows you to do many things for free, such as:

- Free entry to the best museums and attractions

- Free canal cruise

- Free, unlimited use of the GVB public transport anywhere in Amsterdam (this includes the bus, tram & metro)

- A free city map

- Free giveaways & discounts on concerts, theatre, rentals, and restaurants

Now that you have your city card at your disposal, let's have a look at some of the free things you can do in the city.

Start off with a free walking tour

Head over to the national monument to Dam Square for either 11:15am or 1:15pm departure times. There are a number of eager and energetic tour guides willing to show you a glimpse, and while it is free, you are encouraged tip them for their help.

Delve into Amsterdam's city archives

Uncover historic items and unique relics from the archives of The Amsterdam Treasures collection, located in the basement Treasury of the building.

Go on a boat ride with cats

There is a houseboat full of cats, called the

Poezenboot. What is even more awesome is that it's free, though you can make a donation to visit. It's open Monday-Tuesday and Thursday-Saturday, from 1pm-3pm.

Take a whiff at the floating flower market

Down one single canal is an array of flowers—of every color, smell and shape. Visiting the market is free, though you might want to purchase a few while within the vicinity.

Take an amazing panoramic snap at the OBA public library

Okay, so perhaps a library is probably the last place you would want to visit, however this one is very different. Go to the top floor for a breathtaking view of the city.

Learn about weed at Cannabis College

Cannabis College is situated inside a 17th century monument, occupying two floors. Visitors learn all about cannabis, its properties and generally how awesome it is. The college is run by volunteers and admission is free, however if you wish to access their indoor garden then a small donation is required.

Check out Amsterdam's urban beaches

Even though the city is nowhere near a seaside, the Dutch people didn't let that stop them, so urban beaches were created. The city has three to choose from:

- Blijburg

- Muiderlaan 1001 Amsterdam (at this beach you can actually swim)

- Strand West, Stavangerweg 900 Amsterdam

Take an obligatory snap at the I Amsterdam sign

Everyone has at some point online seen the big sign in Amsterdam located in the city's area known as Musuemplein. You might as well join in on the craze before someone takes it away.

Take a casual stroll through the Red Light District

The oldest part of the city, the area has grown to provide sex shops, brothels, gay bars, peepshows, etc. All the things needed for a fun trip with your senior parents. Remember though, pictures are not allowed, so don't take any photos or you will get into some serious trouble.

Go on a mini-voyage

The ferry behind the central station is free and you can even take 3 different routes. During the journey, you will get the opportunity for a wide view of the city's iconic waterfront.

Squeeze into the narrowest house in the world

The narrowest house in the world is in Amsterdam (on the Singel, no.7). The one meter wide house is smaller than an actual front door, though the rear façade of the house is even smaller. It's worth checking out while in the city.

Go skating on a Friday night

Provided it's not raining, every Friday throughout the year, proficient skaters can go on a skate tour through the city (about 20 km) and it is free of charge. You are allowed to join if you are a skilled skater and can handle brakes effectively. It starts at 'the round bench' next to the Vondel CS which is in Vondelpark. Everyone congregates at 8pm for the event so be there or be square.

Take a stroll to the city's infamous Canal Belt

Amsterdam's Canal Belt was recently added as a UNESCO World Heritage site and it is understandable why. Designed and built back in the 17th century, taking a stroll around gives you an insight to the city's history. There are many beautiful Canal Houses lined up on the Herengracht, Keizersgracht and Prinsengracht, with architecture reminiscent of a time when trade was affluent in the city.

Play a game of chess

Whether you are a novice or a pro, you can have a game at the Max Euwe Center. Here you can also learn about the history of chess or play a virtual game. And again, free of charge.

Observe the street art in Amsterdam

You can't escape art in the city, but street art offers more of a motif, usually to highlight a liberation movement through the medium of graffiti. Graffiti is often misconstrued in a negative light, but Amsterdam's street art is on a different level.

The Jordaan area, where art and food collide

Jordaan is Amsterdam's most popular neighborhood, once a working-class bastion known for close-knit communities, sing-a-longs and booze lovers, gentrification has led the area to become more refined with galleries, restaurants and specialty stores.

The Jordaan starts at Brouwersgracht, just west of Centraal Station, and then arches around the Canal Ring between Prinsengracht and Lijnbaansgracht.

Hidden cafes, lucrative courtyards and avant-garde galleries are all synonymous with Jordaan, and you can find them through the area's maze-like streets, and be greeted by street musicians along the way. Here are a few of the best things to do when you visit the area.

Go to the Anne Frank House

Central Amsterdam is known as one of the most historic parts of the city, let alone the Netherlands, but nothing stands out more than the Anne Frank House.

This historical landmark was established in 1957 in the very spot where a bright little girl wrote her iconic memoir, The Diary of a Young Girl. It is recommended to purchase tickets in advance and plan well ahead so you don't miss the chance to visit.

Grab a cocktail or two inside a classy bar

Bar Oldenhof is a haven for tired tourists wishing to escape Jordaan's urban maze. It has an easy-going atmosphere similar to a relaxed jazz club and is a great way to end a day.

Go on the only houseboat museum in the world

Woonboot Museum is located inside a 1914 freighter that was converted into a houseboat. As you go through the canal system, take some time to absorb poignant mementos. This is also only 5 minutes away from the Anne Frank House.

View work by famous painters Picasso and

Matisse

Galerie Buuf is in the heart of Jordaan, and this modern art gallery exhibits many of the neighbor's fine art, as well as vintage collections by Pablo Picasso and Henry Matisse.

Get everything you need at Lindengracht Market

Once a street block of no particular relevance, this is now a bustling marketplace every Saturday. Everything about the marketplace exudes quality. From handcrafted items, cheese, fresh fish, and even snacks, there is pretty much everything available.

Places for kids

According to a report by UNICEF, Dutch kids are the happiest in the world, and if you plan on bringing your little ones out on an adventure in Amsterdam, here are some excellent places to take them for a fun-filled family break.

Go on a picnic at the Zoo

At Artis Royal Zoo, kids can get really close to the animals—practically close enough for a poke, though not advised. The zoo has many things to keep the kids fascinated, such as a small planetarium, aquarium, petting zoo and even a playground. Families can bring a picnic lunch if it's nice weather, otherwise there is a stylish café full to brim with yummy food.

Take the kids to a huge playground

Amstelpark is a magical wonderland not only for kids, but adults as well. Aside from a massive playground and petting zoo, the park also has bumper cars, mini-trains and snack bars too. It's a perfect place to visit on a hot summer's day.

Participate in cooking lessons with your kids

Kinderkookkafé (Kids Cook Café) is a small restaurant that allows kids to cook their own pancakes. Children as young as eight can also sign up to play chef for a day. Kids can also opt to make other dishes such as pizza (and who wouldn't).

Conduct fun science experiments

Ondekhoek (Discovery Corner) allows kids four years or older to choose from 36 different science experiments and activities with little to no parental supervision. You might want to bring a book with you as the kids won't want to leave for hours.

Allow your kids to interact with science displays

NEMO is the largest science center in the Netherlands. There are five floors, jam-packed with exciting things to do and discover for all ages such as workshops, exhibitions, theater, films, demonstrations and kids can learn through touch, sight and sound in most of the activities.

Tours you don't want to miss

Amsterdam's compact, flat and vibrant streets make exploring by foot the most desired approach for sightseeing. From the stunning canals to leafy parks, the city's landscape is a reward in itself, however, there is so much more. If you intend to get behind the scenes with expert guides, then a tour is in order. Here's a few of the best the city has to offer.

For the budding photographer go on Amsterdam's Photo Safari

It's time to put the selfie stick to rest and join professional photographer Tim Collins on his photographic tour of the city. Tim is an expert in finding original locations, whether it's desolate urban landscapes or poignant canal views. You can go on this tour during the day or at night, and anyone is welcome.

A history lesson in WWII and the Holocaust in

Amsterdam

World War II experts Peter Schaapman and Ben De Jong provide visitors an in-depth history into the traumatic period on the tour. During the tour, you will visit all key locations including a trip to the site of the Battle of Arnhem.

Foodie's delight in a street food tour

The Hungry Birds tour gives you the chance to sample some of the city's best street food in the course of one afternoon. Dutch cheese, Belgian fries, spicy spring rolls, pancakes and raw herring are just some of the treats in store. The tour is also available for vegetarians and the price is all-inclusive.

An unexplored street art tour

AllTourNative Tours takes you out of your comfort zone and into unknown territory to tourist-free zones where you will find symbolic street art and graffiti, as well as visit some funky galleries and shops too.

A tour on the masterpiece Night Watch painting

Behind every great painting is a great story and this one is no exception. Jacques Hendrikx, author of a novel about the infamous painting, takes tourists on a journey to the location where Rembrandt painted the Night Watch, and recounts the life stories of the people featured in the painting.

Amsterdam's hidden gem

For over 425 years, Amsterdam was known internationally as the 'City of Diamonds.' If learning about carats, colors and cuts are your thing, then head on down to Gassan Diamond's factory. Tours are free and run from 9 am to 5pm, and are available in over 27 languages.

Check out the largest street market in the

Netherlands

The 'Albert Cuypmarkt' is not only the most famous street market in The Netherlands but also the biggest. The market has been running for almost 100 years, and with over 300 stalls, chances are you will find a thing or two worth buying.

Chapter 4: Where to Stay

Finding accommodation in compact Amsterdam may only take a few steps, though generally visitors start looking for somewhere to stay at Centraal Station before venturing further out. From this point, the city radiates outward in half-circles known as 'the ring.' Most things you plan to do or see are based within the ring. If you plan on just walking around for your duration, the recommended areas to stay are in Centrum and Jordaan. Alternatively, some bolder tourists rent a houseboat for a few nights which is probably something you can't do in other cities. Below is a brief guide to the city's main areas and what they generally entail.

Centrum: one of the most popular spots to stay in the city, full of tourists and short-term visitors. It's close to pretty much everything and is easily accessible.

The Jordaan: A paradise for sophisticated and experienced travelers, hipsters or both, the area is a collection of old and new, with many small streets and canals to charm you.

Canal Belt/Nine Streets: This area is protected by the UNESCO and hasn't changed in over 400 years. If you enjoy boutique stores and quaint cafes, then this is your place.

De Pijp: This area grants convenient access to favorite tourist spots while getting a taste of local life. Loads of shops, cafes, bars and markets will keep you busy.

Museum Quarter: The museum quarter is known for housing many of the famous museums in the city, plus upscale restaurants and resonating Vondelpark. If you are seeking high culture, class and luxury, you'll want to stay here.

Oud West: This area is a mixture of things, diverse and suburban, with a communal feel. If you wish to transition into a becoming local while staying in Amsterdam, here is your place.

Oost: Popular with young families, this residential area is a fabulous place to stay if you have kids. There are acres of green space and it's easy to get around via trams.

Places to Stay on Budget

Backpacking on a budget is nothing to feel ashamed of and on the grand scale of things, you can use the excess money for activities and sightseeing excursions. Amsterdam has many affordable places to suit just about anyone, and here's a select few for your consideration.

Brothel turned hostel

Cocomama Hostel is in a convenient part of the city though it is not as touristy, and maybe that's a good thing. The stylish hostel is very cozy and if you are really tight for money, you should opt for the dormitory. They also have a cat called Joop. The hostel used to be a brothel, but thankfully those kinds of shenanigans occur in private rooms.

Rates: Dorms: €21- €45; Privates: €76- €150

Location: Westeinde 18, 1017 ZP, Amsterdam, Netherlands.

Mingle with other travelers with ease

Generator Amsterdam is a hostel that was previously a zoological building. The old lecture hall was reincarnated into a lively lounge and upbeat bar. The hostel has a game room, perfect for meeting other travelers and making some friends. Located near to the tram stops, and only a few tram stops away from Central Station, Generator Amsterdam is nicely placed.

Rates: A bed in a 4-bed mixed dorm starts at €17

Located: Mauritskade 57, Oost, 1092 AD Amsterdam, Netherlands

Watch a movie in a teepee

Ecomama Hostel is located in the heart of Amsterdam, next to the Jewish Museum and Waterlooplein Flea Market. One of the biggest features of the hostel is its huge communal spaces. You can chill with an unlimited supply of magazines, sip on coffee in their café or watch a movie inside their teepee (yes, a teepee). There are seven different types of rooms to accommodate every type of traveler, and for the budget backpacker, the dorms are luxurious.

Rates: Dorm €27

Located: Valkenburgerstraat 124, 1011 NA, Amsterdam, Netherlands.

A hostel with a library you say

ClinkNOORD is located in Amsterdam's NOORD area (hence the name), and is far from the noise of Central Station or the temptations of the Red Light District. The hostel has over 750 beds, with the dorm rooms housing approximately six to sixteen people, with each bed sports a USB port and light. What makes this place stand out is that it has a library as well as an in-house ZincBar (offering Dutch classics such as bitterballen).

Rates: A 4-6 person mixed dorms start at €24.

Located: Badhuiskade 3, 1031 KV Amsterdam,

Netherlands

Rooms with unusual names and a bar called Kevin bacon

Hotel not Hotel is very unusual, the designs are quirky, vibrant and captivating to say the least and the hotel is all about the design. The rooms were designed by individuals from Eindhoven Design Academy, creating different themes and names such as 'crisis free zone' or 'secret bookcase XL,' and many more. They even have a bar called Kevin Bacon. The hotel is based on Piri Reis Square, walking distance from the tram No 17 stop.

Rates: A shared room starts from €63

Located: Piri Reïsplein 34, 1057 KH Amsterdam, Netherlands.

Upscale Accommodation for when you want to Splash Out

Luxury hotels in Amsterdam are noted for their location, contemporary interiors, world-class service and many other elements. Combining a taste of old-world elegance with modern indulgence. If you are unsure where to find a hotel, then look no further, because here is list to help you pinpoint exactly where to stay.

A hotel consisting of 25 canal houses

The Pulitzer is set on an excellent stretch of the city's most glorious canals, with only five minute walks to landmark tourist spots such as the Royal Palace and Anne Frank House. Some rooms give guests an astonishing view of the many canals, with the rooms decorated with paintings. The hotel intertwines 25 different buildings and since it sits between two major canals, guests can go on a mesmerizing walk through an array of passages, stairways, and open spaces.

Rate: from roughly $150 per night

Located: Prinsengracht 315-331, 1016 GZ Amsterdam, Netherlands

A raw bar and best fish restaurant in the city

Sofitel Legend the Grand is based in the heart of the city, and is close to most major tourist attractions. The hotel's rooms are spacious and beautifully decorated, with designs using natural tones. The in-house restaurant is considered one of the best places to feast on fish, and the hostel also has a raw bar too which is great for health enthusiasts or foodies.

Rate: From $260 per night

Located: Oudezijds Voorburgwal 197, 1012 EX Amsterdam, Netherlands

A Japanese styled hotel with panoramic views

Hotel Okura is as slick and sophisticated as they come, located on the outskirts of the city, predominately within the business district. The hotel boasts a huge lobby that pays homage to Japanese culture. The hostel has 23 floors with each room featuring some stunning panoramic views. Okura also has five restaurants which give the hotel four Michelin stars.

Rate: from $180 a night

Located: Ferdinand Bolstraat 333, 1072 LH Amsterdam, Netherlands

Spend a day at the spa

Built in the 19th century, the Amstel is a classic grand hotel that has retained much of its elegance. Rooms here are furnished with dashes of antique taste, and the best rooms are those that provide views over the river towards the old part of the city. The hotel comes with a 25-meter pool as part of its spa, and the waterside restaurant on the river Amstel is considered of the highest ranking in the city.

Rate: From $300 per night

Located: Professor Tulpplein 1, 1018 GX Amsterdam

Bank turned to music conservatory turned hotel

Conservatorium Hotel wasn't always an upscale hotel, in the 19th century the building was once a bank. The hotel is a three minute walk from the Van Gogh Museum and rooms are equipped with coffee machines. There's also a spa, two upscale restaurants and a pretty nifty bar.

Rate: From $330 per night

Location: Van Baerlestraat 27, 1071 AN Amsterdam

Chapter 5: Shopping

Things you can't Buy Anywhere Else

Amsterdam's unique charm is sometimes hard to put into words but thankfully there are other ways such as souvenirs, gifts and other items. To help you capture the experience of Amsterdam's cultural integrity and diverse history, here is a list of things to buy from the Dutch.

You've heard of calendars but what about a Dutch Birthday Calendar

Getting someone a calendar as a gift seems like the worst present ever, though photo frames are pretty bad. However, the Dutch have something very different instead, a timeless birthday calendar. These are used for recording birthdays and they only have numbered dates. They are found in almost every Dutch house and offer a more personal approach to remembering someone's special day.

Dance while wearing clogs

Who doesn't love shoes, especially those made from wood. They are actually great for walking around in muddy terrain and are as symbolic to the Dutch as their pancakes. The best spot to buy these is either in

Otten & Zn in De Pijp.

Go hunting for cheese

You can't come to Amsterdam and not buy some of their infamous cheese. There are cheese stores scattered all over the city and the most popular cheese varieties (Edam and Gouda) are easy to procure. Other cheeses to consider investing in are Boerenkaas (farmer's cheese), goat's cheese, sheep's cheese and cows' cheese.

Read a copy of Anne Frank's Diary

The diary is one of the most translated Dutch books in history, and you can also find the original at the Anne Frank Museum.

Pick up some Delftware

The delftware factory isn't within walking distance

in the city, however their products are sold in many tourist shops.

Chew on some Liquorice

Licorice is renowned in Amsterdam and it comes in lots of different varieties like sweet, soft, hard and salty; as well as unique flavors, such as strawberry, honey, or melon. You can purchase drop (the Dutch word for licorice) in pretty much any supermarket or pharmacy, the best neighborhood for the candy is in Jordaan.

Give your garden a present

The Netherlands is known for its beautiful tulips, and the bulbs make a great gift. There are other Dutch flowering bulbs to consider as well, so you may want to get a selection on your visit.

A bottle of Genever shouldn't go amiss

Dutch Genever comes in many different forms and flavors to choose from, and the best location to taste the popular drink is at the House of Bols.

Indulge in some Hagelslag

For those of a sweet tooth, Hagelslag is a sure-fire way to satisfy your sugar cravings. They come in various forms such as blue, pink and chocolate, and are usually sprinkled on bread or biscuits at breakfast or lunch.

Purchase some stuff from HEMA

HEMA is one of the biggest Dutch chains and offers everything you can think of. It is known for its brand-less inexpensive clothes and photograph services.

Where to Shop in Amsterdam

Whether you are on a tight budget, or you wish to 'shop 'til you drop,' Amsterdam has it all. The only problem is deciding specifically which area has the majority of things you want. Thankfully we have created a rough guide to help you decide.

Shopping areas you need to visit

There's an entire block to check out at De Negen Straatjes ('The Nine Little Streets')

The picturesque Nine Streets location overlaps Herengracht, Keizersgracht, and Prinsengracht within the Central Canal Ring where you will be greeted with small businesses, cozy cafes, cool art galleries, vintage stores and designer boutiques among other things.

Popular places to check out:

- Episode; a popular and trendy vintage store.

- We are labels; A cool boutique for fashion necessities.

- Brix; a retro café famous for its bitterballen.

Visit the first ever yoga shop, enjoy freshly ground coffee and try out loads of shoes in De Pijp

De Pijp is a mixture of vintage, designer and boutique stores with a strong emphasis on European fashion. This is the type of area where you would plan to get a total makeover. The first ever yoga shop known as 'Zen' resides in De Pijp which sells things you probably didn't even know existed.

Popular places to check out:

- Angel Agudo: A hip men's store that sells Scandinavian and Italian shoes.

- Yogisha: The go-to place for hair treatment and styling products.

• CT Coffee & Coconuts: A former cinema turned coffee shop, baristas grind freshly roasted coffee beans right before your eyes.

Interested in bar hopping, cultural sights and furniture?

Haarlemmerdijk is an eccentric shopping area popular with younger visitors. There are two main streets, called Haarlemmerdijk and Haarlemmerstraat, where you will find many cafes, shops and bars throughout. It's excellent for a pub crawl, or if you just wish to stretch your legs.

Popular places to check out:

• Stout!: A really hip restaurant, stout means naughty in Dutch. You should go there to find out why.

• Restored: For furniture lovers who wish to bring something unique back to their home.

For the luxurious tourist visit PC Hoofstraat

This area hosts mainstream brands such as 'Giorgio Armani,' 'Burberry,' and 'Louis Vuitton' as well as over 160 others.

You can opt to walk through Vondelpark on your way to your favorite fashion brands. The museumplein, a square of the most popular museums, is also located here so you should reminisce on a particular romantic element exploring this area.

Popular places to check out:

Momo: A sushi restaurant like no other, though expensive.

Flowers, familiar fashion and fine dining

Leidsestraat is one of the main shopping streets of the city center. You will recognize popular fashion brands, like 'H & M' but there are also exclusive stores too like 'Karen Millen.'

The square is usually where locals tend to come out to wine and dine during an evening.

Popular places to check out:

De Zotte: A Belgian beer tasting bar, what more could you want.

Fillippa K: An exclusive fashion store found only in Amsterdam.

Spacious shopping and bargain prices in Beethovenstraat

This area was built in the 30s and provides loads of space, both for sidewalk and parking. If you are looking for great cheese or you are a chocoholic, then this is the place. The street has a mix of cheap local stores if you are on a budget.

Popular places to check out:

HEMA: Netherlands version of Walmart but better

quality.

PAUW: Clothing store that's affordable and classy.

Groven+: Hip clothing store that also offers excellent prices.

An Amsterdam shopping guide wouldn't be complete without including the weirder, avant-garde stores in the city. Check out some of these stores if you intend to get a gift that will make friends or family gasp, laugh or smile.

Great gifts for men made by men

Concrete matter sells products orientated towards the average guy and might just be the ultimate gift store for dudes. All products are exceptionally cool such as colorful tubes of shaving foam or outdoor accessories, check it out when you get time.

Located: Gasthuismolensteeg 17, Amsterdam

Unknown brands that are affordable AND a coffee shop

T.I.T.S (This Is The Shit) is a quaint store with an array of funky brands that while are unheard of, look badass. Not only are the clothes at a great price, but there is also a coffee corner where you can opt to drink in their garden.

Located: De Clerqstraat 78

Co-working space meets shopping

HutSpot gives visitors a foundation for creativity, a space to generate ideas, products and meet people on your wavelength. Aside from being able to also shop here for accessories, art and household goods, you can enjoy their café with great sandwiches and a refreshing cup of coffee. This is a great place to work or purchase goods for your own business. All brands use sustainable materials and secure the rights of workers and producers.

Located: Rozengracht 204-210

Workshops on going green and cool accessories at Wildernis

This concept store elevates nature to a whole new level. Inside is like a jungle, but with cakes and coffee. The store offers workshops on how to turn your plants into works of beauty. Wilderness is most likely one of the greenest stores in Amsterdam, if not on the planet.

Located: Bilderdijkstraat 165 F

Chapter 6: Entertainment

Amsterdam holds events and festivals probably more than any other European country and there is always something going on in any given month.

During winter time, there is International Fashion week or a few concerts at Concertgebouw. Visiting a museum is usually best when it's winter if not for the lack of crowds and because it's relatively quiet. There's always the option to go ice-skating on the frozen canals or experience the mesmerizing light festival.

In the spring, things become more animated, especially for the King's Birthday celebrations when everyone dresses in orange for 2 days. There is also the Holland Festival where there is a strong art presence in music, ballet and visual arts.

Amsterdam's summer brings open air festivals, concerts and everyone's favorite event—gay pride.

When it is fall, the city takes on more cultural events such as antique markets, film festivals and museum events. One of the most notorious and important is the IDFA (International Documentary Film Festival) which beings around November.

Free Festivals

There are many festivals in Amsterdam and what makes them even better is that they are free! Please check out a few we have included for your itinerary.

Free festival to mark the cultural season

The Uitmarkt festival has been getting better and better each year and is also the largest in the country. The festival attracts over 500,000 visitors and has 2,000 performers across 30 venues for free. It's held in the Museumplein and Leidseplein areas.

Open Air Theatre for free

Vondelpark hosts an Open Air Festival which includes a three-month program that consists of jazz, cabaret, stand-up comedy and much more lucrative and exciting things. It's held on every weekend during the summer and though free, you can make voluntary donations.

Get your freak on at Gay Pride

Gay Pride is notable everywhere, but in Amsterdam it's unique for its canal parade with colorful floats passing through, and there are about 80 boats. It's usually held around late July and takes place along the Prinsengracht.

Illuminate ideas at the Amsterdam Light Festival

This event has a range of entertaining activities such as a boat tour and a free walking tour, as well as a shopping night. It lasts for around 50 days and there are dozens of breath-taking light sculptures on the water, on buildings, and pretty much everywhere, so you can't escape them.

Dress in orange for the King

On King's day everyone dresses in orange and there are loads of free festivals and events throughout the country. Expect one of the biggest street parties you have ever experienced.

Art Museums and Theatre

Art Museums in Amsterdam

Amsterdam has some of the world's most renowned and famous artists such as Vermeer, Van Gogh and Rembrandt—and with 800 years of historic Dutch art to plow through, you might be wondering about the best places to go. Don't fret, as we have compiled a few of our own favorites for you to consider.

The first place to visit should be the Rijksmuseum

This museum has the largest collection of art and artifacts with all the heavy-hitters, including over 40 paintings by Rembrandt. Here you will find the famous "Night Watch" painting and Vermeers' "Kitchen Maid."

There is a wealth of 17th century furniture to ogle

at and fascinating 18th century doll houses that might spook you too. Prepare to learn about the Golden Age and all the treasures it brought to Amsterdam.

Visit a canal house with modern exhibitions

Foam is a photography museum inside a renovated canal house where there are regular exhibitions. Some of the themes at the exhibitions are thought-provoking, such as crime scene photos or just pictures of famous models like Kate Moss. There are also organized talks and events for those who love photography.

You can't visit Amsterdam without going to the Van Gogh Museum

Van Gogh created over 200 painting during his lifespan and you can find these at the Van Gogh Museum. Aside from an intricate look at the artist's life there are also events on Friday evenings (talks, films and lectures) though these can get busy, so book ahead.

Learn about the Netherlands Jewish community

The Joods Historisch Museum (Jewish Historical Museum) was established in 1987 when four synagogues were converted into the museum. Many of the items on display here represent the rich history of the Jewish people throughout the centuries in the country. Some of the exhibitions are surreal and timeless like the work of Charlotte Saolmon, who tragically died in Auschwitz.

Exhibits that are innovative, fun and well-thought out

While some of the museums in Amsterdam might seem like a drag, the Amsterdam Museum is something else. The exhibits here are presented in fashionable, illuminating ways that will leave a constant reminder about your experience. The history of the city is delivered to you in a modern enthusiastic way and you learn how the last 800 years has shaped the city.

Cinematography that will leave you speechless

The EYE Film Institute specializes in edgy, risqué content that will spark your interest in art again. There's a permanent exhibition space, an education area (which is free) and "EYE" pod screening booths.

Unusual museums to check out:

• Sexmuseum Amsterdam: Sexy artifacts and very naughty art made for fun.

• Torture Museum: Spooky galleries of equipment used to torture people.

• Electric LadyLand: Museum of Florscenet art, a pretty cool glow-in-the-dark experience.

• Kattenkabinet: Art devoted to cats, yes cats. Though some of the work is by Picasso and Rembrandt.

Quirky and alternative theatres in Amsterdam

Theatres in Amsterdam don't abide by commonplace rules that are set in other parts of the world, they are more unpredictable in nature and can be wild. Theatres tend to mix a range of different art forms innovatively creating a unique performance. In essence, theatres are off the beaten track so to speak and so it can be tricky to find a quality performance.

Fortunately to save you time, we have compiled a list from the established to the alternative.

Tradition vs innovation at Toneelgroep Amsterdam

The largest theatre company in the Netherlands, Toneelgroep is known for quality performances that combine many elements of everyday life. The theatre has garnished considerable international attention over the years and has 20 core house actors on their roster, not excluding temporary extras from other established groups. International influences that maintain national integrity yet introduce provocative innovation are some of the key reasons for the theatre's success. Performances are in Dutch, however they are often subtitled in English.

Located: Leidseplein 26, Amsterdam

A milk factory that makes stage productions

De Melkweg (Milky Way) is set inside a former milk factory in central Amsterdam. Established in 1970, the non-profit organization has created countless exhibitions, dance performances and theatre productions. The theatre has a number of well-established actors and directors who yearn to push beyond limiting social constraints, resulting in fresh, experimental and dynamic performances. Going to a show here can be unpredictable, you may end up enjoying it or hating it, but that's one part of its charm. Productions are mostly in Dutch but regularly host in English.

Located: Lijnbaansgracht 234, Amsterdam

Comedy, dance and theatrical performances at De Kleine Komedie

Founded back in 1786, De Kleine Komedie has even had King Willem I and Napoleon as guests. The venue has alternated between lectures and a bicycle lot over the years before becoming a theatre again. The theatre proudly calls itself the oldest theatre in the Netherlands and shows with English are marked 'Language no problem.' Expect a range of different shows and performances from dance, comedy and productions.

Located: Amstel 56-58, Amsterdam

Novice and amateur performers get on the stage for your entertainment or horror

De Engelenbak (meaning Dutch for The Gods) is the balcony above the upper circle of a theatre. Since this is where the cheapest accessible seats are, the theatre's prerogative is that anyone can come. Anyone can get on stage and perform (provided they have some talent). By encouraging emerging talent, the theatre is a stepping stone for amateurs trying to make it into the professional world. De Engelenbak offers productions in mime, opera and cabaret.

Located: Nes 71, Amsterdam

Young performers and seasoned professionals collide

Cabaret, dance and modern theatre productions are some of the highlights of Theater Bellevue. The in-house theatre company focuses on quality performances and many other companies tend to try out their new productions there. Drinks are served during performances and Bellevue attracts a crowds of local professionals as well as curious tourists. Most productions are in Dutch though the host occasionally speaks in English.

Located: Leidsekade 90, Amsterdam

Experimental productions that enlighten and

inspire

Frascati Theater is all about featuring productions from the country and abroad. Though a little pedantic in inviting unknown companies to perform as they wish to maintain a dominant reputation. The general quality of the performances here are ground-breaking and above average. Frascati Theater operates two venues for two different profiles; Nes is for the more established productions while newcomers perform at Frascati WG.

Located: Nes 63, Amsterdam

Located: M. v. B. Bastiaansestraat 54, Amsterdam

Flemish actors take the spotlight

De Brakke Grond is a Flemish cultural institute that works close to Frascati Theatre. Funded and founded by the Flemish government, De Brakke Grond provides Flemish actors and production companies an active role in cultural exchange with the Dutch. The main agenda is incorporating elements of Flemish culture into productions and musical performances, as well as exhibitions, festivals, and debates. Sometimes Flemish films and documentaries are shown here.

Located: Nes 45, Amsterdam

Every performance and act you can think of is at the Koninklijk Theater Carré

Circus acts, ballet, cabaret, musicals, this place has it all. The theater offers a mix of highbrow and low entertainment and art, and has been going strong since 1863. The programs are particularly broad and eclectic, sometimes topical in nature in the form of entertainment, and sometimes more on an intellectual level. The quirkiness is affluent in this theatre and Carré has been known as one of the most popular theatres in the Netherlands due to high demand and reputation for having top acts and trustworthy performances that guarantee quality.

Located: Amstel 115, Amsterdam

Productions aimed for younger audiences

Rozentheater aims to stage productions for young people, enveloping issues faced in their everyday lives, political events and social trends. Performances, poetry nights and open mic are a few of the ways that this is demonstrated with amateur performers, often leading to interesting productions. A large proportion of productions are initiated by young performers or one man shows by young artists. Only a few of the shows are in English.

Located: Rozengracht 117, Amsterdam

And for kids

If you happen to have kids or feel like one, then Jeugdtheater de Krakeling is your theater. Known as the most established children's theatre in the Netherlands, the theater covers a range of entertainment for kids, from puppet shows to performances. Kids aged from 2-17 are encouraged to take part in stage productions in an educative way. Local schools usually interact with the theater for performances.

Located: Nieuwe Passeerderstraat 1, Amsterdam

The main English Language Theater

STET theater stages performances in English and it's the only English language theater in the Netherlands. STET has a range of productions to check out, from cabaret to comedy, dance to drama.

Located: Nassaulaan 17, Wassenaar

A g u i d e t o l i v e M u s i c s p o t s

Live Music spots in Amsterdam

Amsterdam has an extensive collection of bars, clubs and concert halls for music. If there is a type of music you like, chances are there is something for you in the city. Let's have a look at some of the hotspots you should visit when in Amsterdam.

A non-profit styled venue

Melkweg isn't just a music venue, they have cinema, dance and art shows as well and all kinds of music.

Located: Linjbaansgracht 234A, 1017 PH Amsterdam

Local meets global

CC Muziekcafé is a small music pub where anyone can get on stage and perform. The bar is appealing to many for its cozy atmosphere and regular open mic nights.

Located: Rustenburgerstraat 384,1072 HG Amsterdam

Club like feel but in a lounge

Chicago Social Club has a bar open until 4 am every night and a club open three nights a week, attracting both party animals and casual drinkers. The venue is a great place if you need somewhere to dance, but then relax once exhausted.

Located: Leidseplein 12, 1017 PT Amsterdam

Improvised music sessions

Bimhuis is a founding member of the Eurpoe Jazz Network and a venue for improvised music. Inside looks like a black box but the jazz sessions are an integral part to the genre of jazz and jazz lovers.

Located: Piet Heinkade 3, 1019 BR Amsterdam

Contemporary classical music that's a favorite for travelers

Muziekgebouw aan't IJ is only a 10-minute walk from Central Station, with outstanding ensembles, small chamber groups and large orchestras, events here are great for romantic dates.

Located: Muziekgebouw aan't IJ, Piet Heinkade 1, 1019 BR Amsterdam

Volunteer run concert venue

OCCII is very independent, so independent that it is run by volunteers. The venue, located in the Dam, hosts underground and cool music acts. Take a visit to learn more about the underground scene of Amsterdam.

Located: Amstelveenseweg 134, 1075 Amsterdam

Time for some rock N roll

Paradiso is based inside a 19th century religious building, with huge paneled doors. The venue opened in 1968 and was the first rock club in Amsterdam to offer house music nights. Famous people such as Lady Gaga and Al Green have visited the venue.

Located: Weteringscheans 6-8, 1017 SG Amsterdam, Netherlands

Conclusion

Congratulations on making it to the end of this book, and I hope that you are now feeling energized, excited and enthusiastic about visiting Amsterdam.

With this newfound wisdom, you should have an

idea of exactly what you want from the city and where to get it. Here are a few suggestions you could take from this guide:

- Go on a caffeinated shopping spree, try on some clogs and then go to an underground rave.

- Visit a selection of museums and galleries for free then have a picnic in Vondelpark.

- Wander around seamlessly, taking snaps of iconic locations, maybe while riding a bicycle.

- Go to a coffeeshop, smoke some herb and fall asleep next to the I Amsterdam sign. Alternatively just visit the cannabis college.

- Go ice-skating, then on a boat ride and sample some Belgian beers.

- Experience traditional home-cooked Dutch food in a living room restaurant, find a free festival or event and have a coffee in the early hours of the morning.

- Hide inside the smallest house in the world, go to an open mic night and buy a burger from a vending machine.

No matter what you decide to do, I hope this book has helped you a great deal and that you are now well-prepared to head to Amsterdam.

Thank you so much for reading this book. I hope it's useful for you.

If you like the book, would you please do me a huge favor and write me a review on Amazon? I would really appreciate it and look forward to reading your review.

Best

Thomas

Check out my other travel books...

Hawaii
TRAVEL GUIDE

Thomas Leon

Iceland

TRAVEL GUIDE

Thomas Leon